Snow

Also by Martin Anderson

The Kneeling Room
The Ash Circle
Heard Lanes
Dried Flowers
Swamp Fever
The Stillness of Gardens
Black Confetti
The Hoplite Journals I–XXIX
Belonging
The Hoplite Journals XXX–LIX

Snow

Selected Poems
1981–2011

Martin Anderson

Shearsman Books

First published in the United Kingdom in 2012 by
Shearsman Books
50 Westons Hill Drive
Emersons Green
Bristol
BS16 7DF

Shearsman Books Ltd Registered Office
30–31 St. James Place, Mangotsfield, Bristol BS16 9JB
(this address not for correspondence)

http://www.shearsman.com/

ISBN 978-1-84861-212-9

Copyright © Martin Anderson, 2012.

The right of Martin Anderson to be identified as the author of this work has been asserted by him in accordance with the Copyrights, Designs and Patents Act of 1988.
All rights reserved.

Acknowledgements
To the editors of the following magazines and reviews in the Philippines, Hong Kong, Canada, USA, Austria and UK in which these poems, and in some cases earlier versions of them, first appeared: *Antigonish Review; Fire; High Chair; Imprint; Iron; Longhouse; Ninth Decade; O.ARS; Oasis; Other Poetry; Palantir; Paper Air; Poetry Salzburg Review; Prism International; Shearsman; Sulfur; Tamarisk; Tenth Decade; The Graphic; The Journal; Tremblestone; Waves; West Coast Review; Wheatear.*

Thanks to Leung Lo Yu whose help with the translations from Chinese was indispensable.

All of the poems in the collection *Belonging* (2009) were written prior to 2001: hence on the contents page the seeming subversion of chronology.

~

Many of the poems in **Snow** appeared in the following publications: *The Kneeling Room* (Blue Guitar Books, 1981), *The Ash Circle* (Shearsman Books, 1986), *Heard Lanes* (Alms House Press, USA, 1989), *Dried Flowers* (Alms House Press, USA, 1990), *Swamp Fever* (Willamette River Books, USA, 1991), *The Stillness of Gardens* (Willamette River Books, USA, 1994), *Black Confetti* (University of the Philippines Press, Manila, 1999), *Three Poems* (Oasis Books, 2002), *Belonging* (Shearsman Books, 2009).

Contents

from The Kneeling Room
Cockatoo	13
The Pressed Leaf	14
Chichen Itza	15
Schoolgirls	16
The Weaver	17

Uncollected
Blackbird	21
The Pauses	22
To the Tune "Tao Lian Shi" *by* Li Yu	24
To the Tune "Lang Tao Sha" *by* Li Yu	25
Return to the Country *by* Tao Yuan-Ming	26

from The Ash Circle
Horizon	31
Oozedam	32
Distance 2	33
Dufy's La Mer au Havre	34
The Hollow	35
Giorgionesque	36
Rushes	37
Seurat's Port-en-Bessen, the Outer Harbour at Low Tide	38
The Old Russian Quarter, Harbin, North China	39
Snowy Owl	40
Logos	41
To Begin Again	42

from Heard Lanes
Orchid	45
Heather	46

Photograph of my Mother	47
Fossil	48

from **Dried Flowers**

An Urheimat	53
Fobbing	56
Tree Web Leaf River	58
'Esquire'	60
The Theft	61
In Exile	63
Driftwood	64
Dried Flowers	65
Dwarf Pine	67

from **Swamp Fever**

The Source	71
The Pumpkin by the River	72
Three Fathom Cove	73
The Tree	75
Russian Spring	76
The Tallow Tree in Autumn	77
Early Traders in Southern China	78
The Opium Smoker	79
Old Amahs	81
To My Blind Student Reading	82

from **The Stillness of Gardens**

First Frost	85
Corringham	86
The Listener	87
The Call	88
Meeting in Autumn	89
Bonfire	90
The Stillness of Gardens	91

The Destruction of the Summer Palace, Beijing 1860	92
Lotus	93
Indonesian Musicians at The World's Fair, Paris 1899	95
Émigrés	96

from **Black Confetti**

Snow	99
Post-Colonial Memorabilia	100
Holidays	101
Monsoon	102
Clearing Customs	103
In Time	104
City	105
Mises-en-Scène	106
Of Christmases Past	107
Another Country	108
Lux in Domino	109
Maginhawa Street	110
The Stair	111
The Lovely Cow Dung Flower	112
Crepuscular Summer	114
At the 26th University of the Philippines' National Writers' Workshop, Baguio	115

Uncollected

Between	119

from **Belonging**

Light Where There Is	125
A Habitation	128
The Pear Tree	129
Edges	131
A Boyhood	134

Belonging 137
Archipelago Nights 142

Uncollected
from The Fragrant Emporia 149

For Mafruha

from
The Kneeling Room
(1981)

Cockatoo

Melting white
  snow, freshet
    of crest and

feather, from
  boulder to branch
    and into the

air, arabesque
  of water
    that the sun

slowly evaporates
  leaving a white
    trace only, a

vapour, thinning
  in the
    slag of air.

The Pressed Leaf

A leaf, clamped
between pages.

As I take it
out, it flakes

against the air
disintegrates. It

leaves, on both
pages, the print

of its teeth
holding its shadow

up. As, through
layers of rock

it appears
beyond mortality, a

shape, that recurs
again and again

in the packed
layers of tissue

beneath the skull,
a shadow

haunting their
white folds.

Chichen Itza

They raised the sun
here, on maize and

squashes, and put
up emblems in the

night, of sleek
eyed jaguar and

bat, to combat it.
When the cobs

fattened, and the jaws
gripped, they threw

out their hips, and
laughed. Then moved

them wider and
wider, in an

arc, a light on
the trampelled grass

full of quetzal
and parrot feathers

enlarging the space
round their feet.

Schoolgirls

Shiny parabolas
you are fruit. The

undulate air
hangs round you.

Your brown luxuriance
your cottoned gift

exist in the
dull water about

your feet, your
socks turned up

against it, whiteness
measuring us.

The Weaver
(my father at Balnamore Mill, Antrim, 1921)

His toes, under the
water, tapped dreamy
currents, and his
eyes traced the
irregular waifs of
vapour, slim as girls
floating into the vents.
He looked at them
through the window
tapering above the
stream, and there
in dreamy rivulets
the tributary spawned
eels for him. His
eyes, in the fluid
sensual movement
danced. His hands
were lost, in
the slowly emerging
pattern that floated
on the loom.

Uncollected
1981–1982

Blackbird

The yellow billed blackbird
whistles from the blossomed whin

                (9th Century Irish)

That branch   bunched with gold
would heap its treasure on the
listener   if that bird   billed
with yellow   could unloosen the hold
on its throat of centuries   filled
with a tongue that is foreign

The Pauses

        Sound

held   in the ear

      a curved

            insistent shape

the fondled

        neck of a

    jar   moving

  through

      the room   so full

        it seems

to break

　　　　　　　upon the tongue

　　with

　　　　　　　　half of its weight

　　　　　　　　　　　　　else

　　　　　　　　　　where

To the Tune: "Tao Lian Shi" *by* Li Yu

Growing deeper and deeper, my garden is quiet.
And the small courtyard is empty.
The cold beats in on a flurry of washing stones; the wind
        continues.
The long night shrugs its shoulders turns over, but doesn't sleep:
lies awake counting, till a thousand washing stones hammer
        the moon into the curtain.

To the Tune: "Lang Tao Sha" *by* Li Yu

Outside the curtain rain sighs down.
Spring: washed out word, feeling.
Fifth watch. Wind a knife through blanket.
In dream, forgetting the body was captive,
engorged with wine and music.

Alone in the evening, lean on the balcony.
Rivers and mountains roll on and on, without limit.
What we are parted from dare not ask when we'll meet again.
Dropping flowers, rushing water, spring. Gone.
Far, unattainable country.

[Li Yu, 936–978 CE, was the last emperor of the southern Tang dynasty. Captured and taken north to the Sung capital and placed under house/palace arrest, he was forced to take poison for allegedly, in a line in one of his poems, appealing for the restoration of the Tang dynasty]

Return to the Country *by* Tao Yuan Ming

I

I was not born to the world's music.
My being was ground in hills and mountains.
For thirty years I breathed the din;
it toiled and choked me.
Trapped birds pine for the trees.
Pond fish long for wider waters.
In the south I broke open wild edges
returned to these hard farmlands
with ten or eleven acres, a house
and a few straw huts to sustain me.
Elms and willows flood eaves with shadow.
Out front the courtyard is full
of pear and peach trees.
A village greys in the distance;
a soft spoil of smoke hangs over its market.
Dogs bark deep in alleys.
Cocks crow in mulberry bushes.
These houses and courtyards
are deaf to the world's music.
A bare room accumulates space to think.
For years a net hung on my sight.
Now I return to what's within me.

II

Nobody of importance ever comes to this place.
Our dead-end lanes echo only to the rattle of one harness.
Doors stand half open in day's clear light.
In bare rooms thought gathers no dust.
In cloaks of woven straw sometimes, returning
from market, we meet in lanes.
When we meet we talk, but our talk is always free of gossip.
Mulberry and hemp keep it pure.
Every day the mulberry and hemp on my acres prosper.
Always, though, I am afraid that frost and hail
will level everything and drive me back to wild grass again.

[Tao Yuan-Ming, 372–427CE, the poet of quietness and solitude.
Of his poetry the great Sung dynasty poet Su T'ung-Po wrote:
"There is no poet I treasure more … He wrote few poems: they are
plain yet beautiful, rich and yet not ornamented. Tu Fu, Li Po and
all the others are inferior to him".]

from
The Ash Circle
1986

Horizon

Curve
                        transparency
          fold
                            of effulgence
air
            the mind
        closes on
                          appetent
                                    pre-
occupied
                Gloss
      that moves   through
                its tear

Oozedam

          Saltings
    wiers of silt
               bleach
     ing stones
The river cracked
   to a dry whisper
  in the grass
Far out   the gleaming fleet
     withdraws
  light
         distance
   breaking upon itself
  like glass
        Under it
the vanished fields and walls
                 listen
     The forests of ash
  open their scars

Distance (2)

      At its petrified edge
        the tree
    can go no further
                    A furious white
breath   erases its leaves
         its rings
     At the heart
   of the stone   a mist
      spreads
            There are no doors
there   or windows
      Only   opening onto itself
      the mind
's terrified cry   The light
     of it
         dispersed

Dufy's *La Mer au Havre*

Deep blue   simulates

                *

Mind   Restored
       to itself
    Its tremulous   mask
         its oils

                *

                     Outside
two   blue klaxons
      blow   and pass

The Hollow

      Tight   in the eye's corner
          this gold   this beating
horizon   that's spawned
    further and further
       and   through the hollow
            the lust
  re at the tip of
 the tongue   breathes
  in the rippled
corridor
   the palpitant room
an unease
        Grey as ash
       bright as fire
  within the walls
          Our unexcavated speech

Giorgionesque

Woven   through the flesh
     this gold dust
     this thread   In the black
      folds   of the cypress
    its filaments spin   They
      are pulled   through
     a white dusk
   into this glistening rain   this
      vermilion   the 'ground
of the flesh'   that is breathing
     under the lip of
    the sarcophagus   into
       our name

Rushes

       In muscled
  air   the shudder of
     italic stems
                Tissue
in   its ambulant dress
                  Its super
    fluity
          (within the wind
       's wantonness)
           to which we
bend   Our other
    ness

Seurat's *Port-en-Bessin,*
the Outer Harbour at Low Tide

        Silence

                  flat

tened encomium

                         flow

of escutcheon

     stone   latitudes

       emptying

themselves   evacuated

      streets   the load

          ed   horizontal

The Old Russian Quarter, Harbin, North China

    Tiered kokoshniki
draped with snow   Leftover
  borscht   The stones
of the streets point north

      In the silence
of deserted rooms   the striated breath
  of the crystal
forms   on walls

      Tremulous above pilastered domes
of a church   the eye of a glass angel
  in the grey wind off the tundra
slowly   thaws

Snowy Owl

      Two eyes   float
          on a tumult
of air   above a sharp
   -ly incised breath
                  Feather and bone
      torn apart
drip   Through the trees
    lighter
  whiter   than an afflatus
      it rises   hiss
ing
            Around its neck
       small
   globules of blood   glisten
          Beneath
        them
  twitching intestines
                freeze

Logos

Up and up it comes
through crushed granite
on this loosening
stammering
stairway of sound
It pauses
light
stepping through
a leaf
as it slides
through the tongue
and
with a rattle
of black quartz
and ashes
streams
in a white
humus
toward
the   stars

To Begin Again

   The light of
        place   the eye
  's light   The green
          pulling space
the secret snow   Behind us
they wait
               They fill
     with a cold
     aqueous light
                 the stones
        They sing
under our hands
                    They turn
       all of the afternoon
            all of our ruminations
   white

from
Heard Lanes
1989

Orchid

Fragile bloom
of the ephemeral,
above the lime tip
the bee bites
the voluminous tissue
of your lip
and mounts you;
rubs
until the seed grips
his back, then,
breathless/palpitant,
glides over the long luminous slide
of your shoulders
and leaves you.
In the summer's
deep fecundity of air
you wait,
ovary twisted
under a leaf,
for the amorous wind
to deceive
again and again
with your curves
and projections
to delicately pivot
him
     down
into your nectarious shadows
     there
to swim
against your stigma
     eyes covered
with the fine dust

of an infatuation;
 intoxicated,
   unable to rise.

Heather

Above the bleached grey podsol
it blossoms.
The hill
is awash in an afterglow
of minerals,
chrome
nickel and cobalt.

Anthers,
soft bells
on a wave
of intense blue,
through sandstone
    gravel
                loosen

the light
that in hard pans
burns up
through their dark roots.

    Reveal
the slow
        festering
of metals.

Photograph of my Mother

In the light's
shuttered immobility
you breathe

for this loved body
the air parts
its luminous shadow
and waves.

Amorous
funereal
halogens click.

Through the alchemy
of metals
a dry day
a still
centre
a voluptuous
music.

You pose.
The noise
of Time
bell/clock/watch
breaks
into your heart.

A hard
white gaze
emanates
from your hands
and feet.

Behind you
your bones
speak.

Fossil

The blue dust
of stars
in our bones,
rock,
a dark door
opening,
crumbling
among the lichens.
In a clear pond
the drowned molluscs
and the wasps
are falling,
and falling.
Free of us
at last
our bones tumble
down the long shaft
of our blood.
We listen.
At the dark
well-head
we cannot hear them
drop.

from
Dried Flowers
1990

An Urheimat

Down washed out roads
they walked
into thin air,
they vanished.
Dark vocables,
obliterated voices.

.

Fierce wall of ice
upon the Taurus
mountains.
Clink of a cob's hoof
beneath it.
The unspoked wheel
turns and turns
the trundled cart
leaving behind it
such spaces;
wind blown escarpment
lake.

.

From field
to field
each glittering syllable
each culm
intact
in that slow wave
that advances.

.

What the hand transcribes,
pure white margin
drinking the weight
of these letters
one by one,
walking out of a high
Anatolian light.

.

Ghost of a word
under the tongue.
From its succulent stem
dem
domus
the *house*
rising.

.

Slender grey mouth
of stone.
Each consonant
and vowel wedged
against the dead
post frame
that rotted
and has gone.

.

Word
under the corn
feldspar
iron and bone.
Stippled bracken,
broom
where the burr
of the *r*'s sweet
on the air.
Bloom
through each deliberate
rustle
of sheath and glume.
Bring,
through tremulous ear
and tongue,
through this dark
spoliated tract
of migratings and siftings,
finally,
us home.

Fobbing

Marsh scrub:
flag and rush
bittern, plover.
Among it argent
and gule of Jute buried
under thick coverts
of thorn and gorse.
Here,
in the first assart,
among felled willow
and uprooted aster,
they raised a chapel.
Beneath its ragstone
and flint walls
unculled by wind, centuries
the bull-sedge
(*bula-secg*)
spreads.
Shaggy, bearded
upon banks
of slithering silt
it grips,
in its hard sound,
a rush
of haltered nasals and plosives
bound taut as withes.
With them they made,
above the cord grass
and the trapped salt,
here,
where their shadowy form
rasps and clicks

upon our tongue
still,
a second clearing.

Tree Web Leaf River

The river breathes
in its grey penumbra
beyond the tilted dark
curlicues of the trees.
There is a writing
on the window.
Syllables, sounds that have
not been heard before.
The tethering gold
of the web under the eaves,
the leaf's (pinned
to its shadow on the wall)
thin frail tributary
of veins, inscribe
the silence with
their names: the intricate
entablature that evolves
round them, potent
vibrating. Behind them,
at sloping desks, down
the long afternoons
of summer, stand doors
that open into the years.
A child steps through
them, pronouncing word
after word,
like a catechism, turning
the page of a gradual
and permanent erasure.
One day he will
look back, and try
to open them. To
touch, through the pale

residuum of its sound,
fricative and plosive
loose on the wind,
that grey, quivering
shadow again, faded cunabula
beyond the trees.

'Esquire'

Forlorn,
derelict,
brambles growing through
its trellis of
archaic sound,
up the crunching gravel
of the ear
by the wide lawn
it stalks,
under faded bunting
and flags.
Partridges haunt,
with plump grouse,
the soft moors
of its slopes.
From its lost halls
and dining rooms
the butler
and the valet call.
All the foxes stand,
as its shadowy catafalque
lurches past,
to attention.
Each one raises
a mauled paw.

The Theft

Stared into, never entered.
Behind the wrought iron gate,
the high stone wall.
Through summer after summer
the high chestnut swung
above it, and dropped
without a sound. Propped
on the wall he listened.
Behind the undulant wave
of lace, in the deep
bay window where the glint
of book-spines fired each wall,
their voices rose on a
sonorous curve, and fell.
Amid the delicate clink
of china he strained
to hear their low proprietorial
syllables form in long
involuted sentences. His breath
held. Plenitude of sounds,
of pauses, of the high
superordinate word. Through it
the coriander and the tall columbine
of the wide border twined
their vines, each species
and sub-species, *Camellia japonica
Punica granatum*, into his ear.
Silently, through long nights,
when snow fell against the doors
and windows and covered
the fields, and the clothes-
horse sweated in the front room,
he intoned them. Gradually,

week after week, month
after month, before the mirror
where he moved his lips
leafing the large lexicon
that he'd bought, nasals
that had been inaudible
were noticed, plosives
that were always unaspirated
exploded. Upon his tongue,
beneath high summer moons
among lanes, a clear mellifluous
water, a freshet of fricatives,
began to roll onto the air.
He smiled. Behind walls,
shrined in their arbours
before sundials, boughs
grew heavy with the golden
leafing of new words
and sounds, through which he drew
an intricate harmony, an
interlocking music. The rotundity
of its shadows enveigled his mouth.
And, from the deep garden,
he inhaled their scent.
Each slow, scrumped vowel
inscribed in the air
its perfect circle of breath
aqueous, vibrating.
A soft, voluptuous alphabet,
angel of letters and of impressed seals,
swam; an uncalumniated
dream of caramelised apples
                          inside his head.

In Exile*

My children too have learned a barbarous tongue.
                    Tu Fu.

At that fragile frontier of signs you stop,
and listen. Grief: at the heart ripped out,
the cranium gouged off on the roads. Chang'an.
As you lower your head to read the dusk
slowly expands across the river.
Snow falls, out of a dead sky. Poetry.
Crows tearing the flesh of horses
dead in the shafts, driven too hard, after
so many hurried farewells on the painted terraces.
Smoke devouring the city, where the lotuses
turned red all summer, where the censers never went out.
From dark alleyways and courtyards, now,
its noise drifts through the moon's pale light,
broken, cacophonous, across the river.
Above your desk the blood stained shadow
of the lotus moves its slow, ineradicable
wreath of leaves. You write.
In the snow's fallen silence, a hundred years
of the saddest news; a road for none but the birds.

*(In K'uei-chou on the middle Yangtse where Tu Fu went in 766 CE when the rebellion of An Lu-shan drove him south from the capital Chang'an.)

Driftwood

In the frozen heart
    of a glacier
the top
    of a truncated fir
whitens, gleams:
    in an airless glaze
its twisted boughs
    held up
in an avalanche of crystal.
    They move
without moving,
    in that silent
windless place.
    As they lurch,
year by year,
    down the valley's
plundered slopes
    their fragile tendrils break
like glass.
    A floating effigy
with no leaves;
    a candelabrum
that creaks.
    Over the deep
bedrock, in the vast dark
    of the basal ice,
it lights
    nothing.

Dried Flowers
(*i.m.* D.B.A.)

And nothing now
  to give you
more, or less,
  than was customary,
always,
  between us
than these
  so minutely proportioned
against the dark
  that consumes you
and memory and the light
  of the days—
attenuated
  taut peduncles,
calyxes of fire
  that will burn
on, without water
  rustling the tongue
of a cool
  unideological morning.
Naming for you
  such assurances and reassurances
that I speak
  and, in that activity, seek
the long looked for
  immobility, the repose
(not yours)
  of these flowers
that were wild once.
  That the heat dried
for your tears
  and to be

nothing if not curious
   angular to the touch
of light, of air.
   Turning each day
small, and smaller,
   the spaces of love
between us:
   until they are as rare
ified and pure
   as time is to us
for whom time is not
   ever to be
eradicated or abjured.

Dwarf Pine

   Sun burnt
fosse, dry rattle
  of pebble
above shale.
   Scarps tremble
under the grip
  of snow, ice.
They slowly rot,
  and are held,
where the eye
  gathers
them in cloud,
  and the long
limestone scar twists
  above the crevice's
jagged throat.
   On thin beds
of eddied sand,
  too,
bent grey
  stunted
the dwarf pine,
  in sheer shadow,
pushes
  small
immaculate
  yellow stamens
into cold air.

from
Swamp Fever
1991

The Source

Under hands
the stones palpitate
as if the heart was

in them. Primed
and pulsed at
the earth's core

a streak of red
granite runs through
them. The hands

touch it, fingering
like a spoor
its weaving dark.

The Pumpkin by the River

   Boughs turning over
you, water under
  you. You eat

  your heart out
like a flame
  as if to

  tell me. I
should know, from
  the heat in my

  hands, what it
is, what makes
  the flesh a vapour.

Three Fathom Cove

    Plunge the
mind in, through

    the grey
wave, to this

    wet pit.
Here, three

    fathoms down
in soft black

    shale, the flattened
fossils lie.

    Between each
dyke, in a

    deep sleep, they
coil, eating their

    bands of sediment
listening, year

    by year, to
the slow fall

    of the coast.
Their fine

    white skeletons,
their sharp

edged teeth,
Cephalapsis, Iguanodon,

wait to inherit
the earth.

The Tree

The root is
knotted in
the bank, tied

through it
like a shoelace,
pulled, till the

clay has bulged
into it
bright as blood.

The limpid
green of leafage
shows nothing above.

A dark burl
whorls in
the trunk, thickens.

At its
centre, the light
springs out.

Russian Spring

Each door in the house
gaped. You
broke in, immense and

yawning. They hammered
brackets, soaked the
wall outside with pitch

starred in a diurnal
explosion. Trees dragged
their roots, and neighbours

left vast chairs for you
and chattered under the
thatch. The water

butt drank dry the
canal, and the apples
turned red in the street.

The Tallow Tree in Autumn

In the afternoon
   the light

slips out
   of its gently

waving body
   and is gone.

Leaf and
   stalk are

buried in
   shadow. Inside it

the fat
   white seeds of

the capsules
   hold their own

candle, and
   the sugar pumped

sap reddens
   to a burn.

Early Traders in Southern China

Beneath camphor
    and banyan
in the bright
    sun, their names
'Jardine', 'McMurdo'
    incise the marble
with a burr.
    It rolls upon itself
like water.
    Their hard, metallic
eyes groan
    like the breakers
on that
    northern shore, grey
with its damp
    longing. Their
opiumed fingers are
    scutched white
as cloth.
    In denuded
linoleum parlours
    the sound
of a wasp
    keeps rising.
Night and morning
    it sucks
the pewter light
    above the door.

The Opium Smoker

Under his small
nostrils the
powder burns.

He heaves
and snores, his
ribcage rising

to enclose it.
On the
window the hot

sun whitens
like a coal.
Squeezed from

his lips
a frayed grey
plume drifts

in it.
As they tremble
above his

trunk's thin
folds of
skin, his rattling

throat, the
incubus passes,
blown through

a small ring,
a tightening circle
of silence.

Old Amahs

At corners on
winter mornings, the
amahs come out

for *haw fun.
Their eyes are
full of summer

evenings. Their min-laps
are buttoned tight.
In their pockets

the tram-car tickets
are faded and
curled up. Lodged

there since summer
the balls of
camphor have melted

away. Moths have
ravaged the sleeves
and linings, entering

them like explosions
leaving white puffs
of cotton behind.

*(A type of noodle sold by street vendors)

To My Blind Student Reading

   You move
your hand over
     a frost of

    paper, and
touch the
      papuled letters.

  They rise below
your fingers, and
    slowly mouth themselves.

  Their pressed out
meanings, where
   your eyes

  can't go,
are glimmered in
    the fall of words

   that slowly, softly
in your mind
    are settling

   like fresh
foot prints
    over the snow.

from
The Stillness of Gardens
1994

First Frost

    This morning
a lighter
    light than light itself
like sea/horizon.
    Behind curtains
it waits.
    Stillness
of mineral, opaque
    silence. As if,
in this hush
    of air, the elements
are encouraging us
    to write
on the blank pages
    of our lives
again, the names—
    of morning, of light:
how to pronounce
    upon our tongues
that fragile
    white intensity
of their touch,
    their shape
as the eye perceives
    it leaning out to
wards what is not
    the mind only but
light, morning
    the first frost.

Corringham

Soft gurgle of water under my tongue.
The warm latch in my palm
opens. Here is a name
I can't pronounce. A tall tree
burns in its shadow. A house
of shutters, of diffused fragrance,
stands back from the road.
In the silence of its corners, under
its stairs, in cupboards, there is
a rush of air. Inwards, the field
breathes, inwards. A dark flame
topples towards me. In its bed
of fronds, the deep garden exhales
the secret of glass, of windows

The Listener

For you who are listening.
The locked cupboard in the wall.
The dust behind the wireless
on the floor where you sit,
amassing its silence. Valve glow.
Cursor streaming through light
of all those far away places. Names,
names, enveloped in static, words
across dark spaces. Outside
the snow falling, in the empty garden.
The gate squealing on its hinges.
It is you. Through all the years
drifting, you come back to greet me.
This small echo I hold in the ear
of the world, cupped intransigence,
the voice of a child, talking to itself
in a room of shadows; valve
glow, the warmth of materials—wood,
glass, metal—a transcending
odour, drawing me near
to that conversation that does not end,
to that dark flower, that glass of
imperishable water, from which I drink.

The Call

  Through a storm
of static, sand
  in air,
I hear at last
  your voice.
My ear pressed,
  for so long,
to the edge
  of silence, space
takes time
  to clear. Then
far off,
  behind you
the high, thin wail
  from a minaret
calls, through
  each filament of glass,
out of immense
  distances,
shifting endlessly
  between us,
all the faithful
  to prayer.

Meeting in Autumn

Like a fire died down and almost gone
out, the dulled gold of the leaves above
the water. The brimful depths are listening
to us as we stroll by, arm in arm, and talk
in leafy willow shadow. Scuffed at our feet the lip
of the bank of the canal. Meadow grass,
level and lustrous and lost
in that reflection that records upon itself
our own hesitant progression. The hour hand
laps the second hand in a sweep of fire. Sun,
amplitudinous on arms and hands and faces.
In the dry stone shade of a high wall
we stop, and kiss. Fragrance of leaf mould
on your cheeks, your hair, your lips.
Moss and fern above your head leaning
over to touch us, as I feel my pulse
your pulse, and hear under our feet the crack-
le of dead leaves, smell the thin plume of dust
as we move, rise into the air
to ignite, with your soft fingers and
your tongue, through all weathers here, our passing.

Bonfire
(*i.m.* R.A.)

Silence drifts through your bones
like lead, dragging the smoke out
of the sky. Your eyes smart
as they stare into that flame
that ignites dried piles of leaves
dead stalks and twigs, the debris
of a summer. I catch you,
for an instant, as you turn
and squint, and try to hold
that look across the blurred
lines of all the years
that have passed. At the end
of a garden, now, someone is
raking and piling leaves. I listen –
for that false summer, mind begotten.
It crackles. It turns to a cinder.

The Stillness of Gardens

We inhabit the stillness of gardens,
all our lives. Where the light
turns the pages of a silence
that listens. Where through
its slow dehiscence and exhortations
we try to touch, like touching a shadow,
a place we were born into but
outgrew. A quiet encirclement
of leafage sways in the margins;
a whisper, of warm showers;
a flickering light on walls. Imperfectly
remembered now, imperfectly
construed, they drift at evening
through our empty rooms.
We sit in the shadows, listening.
A bird sings, in the silence.
Like a latch opening within our
minds, a door entering into
a forgotten afternoon, its sound;
like the rustling leaf of a page
(smudged calligraphy, blossoming thumb)
we'll read and re-read the rest of our lives.

The Destruction of the Summer Palace, Beijing 1860

In the Chinese garden the internal boundaries were made vague or ambiguous, time was made to stop and space became limitless ... it was a place apart ... free from the cares of men.
—Maggie Keswick.

After the conflagration of finials, a shout.
The *Rhus Vernificera* turned white.
A cambric sleeve melted in a hand.
The water in the moat dried to a dark stain.
Amid the heat and crackle of ebony galleries
the indigo of landscapes dripped and ran
down into the artificial lake.
All night they lay awake in their tents,
Coldstreams and Grenadiers, coughing
under the pall of a sooted moon.
In the charred ear of corn the reveille echoed,
and echoed. Through the wafted smoor
of rain they rose, their cloaks lichened with
damp ash. On their cheeks a dark stubble bristled.
Before them, insouciant imperial lions
glared from their singed plinths.

Lotus
(Chi Pai-Shih 1863–1957)

In your sleeves
the silence
of crickets

the small
dry spaces
where you lean

your head

to watch
the lotus bloom

How smoothed
and pliant
the air

there   You
have entered it
as you would enter
a small
sunlit room
hesitantly
on quiet feet

And you have
left it
as you found
it uncrumpled
made
out of the silence
that sings

without a line
or a shadow
out of place
but proportionate to
what you observed

a small
chaste repository
a home
for the birds

Indonesian Musicians at The World's Fair, Paris 1899

What rite that passage through innocent seas
would launch, what mud, what agony would accompany
its longing for older, far-off shores
where, from under the banana and
the mango tree, from under that steep
blue Balinesian sky, they beat
with a furious delicacy the air, the force
of their percussion caught in the ear
of Europe, as it sat and listened
and waited—waited, and waited, till it
knew that something was being abandoned.
A melody in fragments, unable to go home.
Dark pastoral. Cobblestone through a window.
All the bells in the belfries of each small town
tolling the fading Angelus. Outside, a crazed
wind in the trees, tearing up the score.

Émigrés

A small room, full of
light and birdsong and
stillness, we cannot step out-
side of. Here, we are our own
echoes. We metabolize
behind windows, all the dawns
of our past life flowing into
this space, all its successes
and failures. Journeying
homeward, we are lapped
by the shadows of an infinite
nostalgia: calls
on the air, from roads,
from bridges. They lead
nowhere. They pass through
us, like the lost rooms
and gardens of our childhood.
We stand here, and listen
to them. Heartbeat. Traffic.
Lost in stillness. Our feet have
wandered to another place. Already
our bodies are embraced by
its sly oblivion, its distance.

from
Black Confetti
1999

Snow

Over the quietness of a far lane
and field, I know you are falling
through a debris of bones and cans,
unaware of how I pronounce the name
of what it is you are. Indifferent:
etiolated. From my cool lexicon
of air you are expelled, onto
a coloured earth that holds you.
As silent as the drift of smoke, of
light, of our secret selves. Fugitive.
You fall through my fingers
with a lightness of breath whose
only sound is a sound I cannot hear,
but imagine. I listen, patiently.
And, slowly, through the quiet shift
and slough of syllables, there is snow,
unexplained, unpronounced, falling
on gate and window. In my mouth
I have formed a silent O to catch it.

[Hong Kong, 1994]

Post-Colonial Memorabilia

Like faded graffiti on walls, these names
of other streets, other roads: Old Bailey, Arbuthnot,
Blenheim. And this light that reflects
from the palm; slow, numismatic.
On the perforated postal order; on the embossed red
crown of the postbox; on the *On Her Majesty's
Service* envelope. The inauthentic dream departs,
taking with it a packing case of mementoes and
insignias, the sound of a leaking memory
of phrases infrequently used, poorly pronounced.
To resurrect, on the other side of the world,
what's 'lost', what's gone … another nostalgia.
Leaving, in its place, an afternoon
finally confirmed in its own right, on its own terms.
The signposts all pointing one way.
The roads and the promenades always
coming back in their sweep to this low
scorched promontory and, on smoke wreathed jetties,
fragrance of incense at makeshift shrines.

[Hong Kong 1996]

Holidays

Light trapped in a shutter;
hosanna of horizons. As we drift
up the last hill, idling
at the top, to silently gaze
on the anticipated immensity inside us.
Edge, falling off into a space
that is endless. High call
of the merganser. Air
of salt washed into our eyes.
A wave dreams against a head
land of crystal, somewhere
behind an embankment. No snapshot.
No souvenir. No memento. Adrift
on the deep insurgency of our shadows.
The restlessness of centuries ignites
quietly in the heat. In our bones.
The smoking hoof:
beat of migration. A rhythm that translates
through us into the light. Superscription
of years we cannot forget.
Shimmer of long, far off horizons.

Monsoon

Crackle of surfaces, of dry air.
Dusty imbroglio. Contracting
and jolting the frames of windows,
stropping the humid warp
of paper. From far north,
across the sands of the Gobi,
gathering, for us, such limpid
pools of light. Our shadows drink
from them. Through the tombs
of the Ming emperors
it blows. Through corridors
of cold stone, touching our hands,
our coats. Soughed in the tilt
of grasses. Its thin, high note
a love cry through our rooms.
Altering invisible compasses.
Strengthening, slowly,
that irrepressible current in our veins.
Through the leaves of the cinnamon
and the pepper trees it rattles,
over the granite wharves beneath the hills
and the torn whitecaps on the bay.
As we lean into it, we breathe
the unmistakable aroma of capsicum;
the fierce fragrance of a dream,
its fine white powder ground
in a mortar, drawn through an alembic
of high wind and sea, of broken spars
and stunted masts, doldrums and calenture.
It hovers here, round these calm headlands.
Amid the stale residue of our lives, it is reefed.

Clearing Customs

After the drone of monotonous interrogations, to pass out
into the heat of abundant foliage, lemonade stands,
tin roofs under papayas. How can one declare
that of which one is still so innocent. Reading in bed,
in strange hotels. Scouring the shelves of bookstores
for an inventory of shadows, an atlas well annotated
by those who have passed here before. To dissect
loneliness fill in your name and address, on endless forms.
And observe the light, how, rising or descending upon
your skin it enters a transparent country you have traversed,
but do not know. The monstrous farrago
of its impedimenta defeats the senses. So we go
into this moist night full of objects inscribed
with our delusions. The indecipherable mystery of who we are.
And, from the strangeness of its fabrics, the unfamiliar
torsions of its smiles, we subtract ourselves and
the vanity of our possessions. To leave, in the heat
of its fierce tableau, the fume of an enquiring look.

In Time

The articulateness of roads. Recovering the sound of their speech.
Smooth as deceit, turbulent as terror. Their note a continuous
    reverberation
on which we are travelling, modulating from asphalt to earth,
leaving behind us, in the fumes of the noodle factory, in the frenzy
of the slaughterhouse and the dead river behind it, the smell
of time. Rising, with a clear tropical light, *liwanag ng araw*, on
their hard shoulder. We hear, in their monotony, the mileage
of our accelerated desires, the promiscuousness of boundaries.
We ride them, weightless for a moment, listening,
over bridges, beside water, to how we move from one
part of ourselves to another, questioning their sly camber,
the way the distance glimpsed at their centre is like the silence
of empty rooms, and the way the wind rustling their verges
throws into our voices a far away accent and pronunciation of
    longing
for what we will, we know, in time, grow tired of and discard.

Liwanag ng araw: Tagalog for the brightness of day.

City

The great stained boles of coconut trees on its flooded
sidewalks peel and fray. Their shadows macerate.
Uncontrite, infected waters seep into its river
where they swell. In its markets at dawn
pale ubod roots are piled high in baskets
beside flyovers; displaced families beg in the fumes
of traffic. Massive realty hoardings above the roads
advertise the joys of country living—fresh air and views.
At the airport and wharves those emigrating gaze sadly back.
Its airwaves are full of the grammar of distance.
White walls of adobe blaze under malls. Metallic discos
thud in suburbs. The track marks of the
last rebellion are still visible on striated curbs.
Dark and igneous, a volcano showers a fine ash
over rooftops. The voices of its women are beautiful
through long nights when the turbines of its generators
uselessly whirr. In the ruins of their eyes streets
and alleyways are transformed into a maze of paths
that flower. Satellite dishes slowly rotate to receive
signals of earthly iniquity. In its bus stations
clouds from millions of journeys gather and are dispersed.

Mises-en-Scène

At the corner of Nakpil Street and Adriatico a boy
half trots balanced between two dripping translucent blocks
of ice, water that's still that flows between the arms
of embracing calipers. A warm, procreant wind gusts.
The downpour long over, the roofs of drying shacks
smoke like embers. At the intersection of del Pilar and Quirino
Avenue, oblivious to traffic, a child a-squat on the sidewalk
repeatedly decants from one paper cup into another
with a mesmerised look a stream of the clearest, pure water.
Like a bracelet around her ankle, a dark betrothal,
flies gather round a wound. And a taxi driver
approaching the end of his twenty four hour shift, his engine idling
in shadow down an alleyway near her, furtively draws the thin
white dust of shabu, as white as snow, into his nostrils.

Of Christmases Past

2 am ... And the wind outside
is piling drifts. A white surplice
thrown over the hedgerow. A silence
at the edge of fields. Noiselessly
someone steals in, then out
of the bedroom. 3 am ... That white
electric glare, defying sleep
and darkness, lighting impatient
hands at gifts. Now, no one
steals in, and I have no room
to steal to. But, sometimes, when
suddenly awake at 3 am,
I stumble through an absolute
stillness, and glare of light
strangely luminescent, to reach
a room that is not there.
Banana and papaya trees loom outside.
The air is hot. I stand, for one
moment, in the immense darkness
beyond the window. High up,
the moon's grey sliver glistens.
Light pools at my feet
in the cold, hard mineral of reflection.

Another Country

Late afternoon sun gilds the sacristy of Malate Catholic Church.
Through the trees sash and surplice drift, against
the gleam of polished pews. The heavy gold doors of the
Grand Boulevard Hotel slowly revolve. Aromatic day.
Huge, explosive encrustations of frangipani sweeten
the air. The fragrance of sesame cakes, from a vendor,
floats. Beside the road, their feet stirring the rubble
of the sidewalk, three girls perch on a narrow wooden trestle.
Bar-whitened faces, dead-end downturned looks. Their eyes move
from side to side, up and down, then out over to the sere grass
of Remedios Park, where a glittering wave on the bay
unloads its light. Behind them, in the sanitized glare of
Dunkin' Donuts, tourists eat. They wait. The damp
wind of a dusk begins to linger in their hair. The fumes of jeepneys
stalled on Mabini invest their clothes. A bride and groom rehearse
through the trees, their fateful walk. Flicker of gold on the finger.
A young tourist with a half eaten doughnut in his hand
comes out, and begins to talk. 'Paraiso, parang ibang bayan.'

Paradise is another country: a Tagalog saying

Lux in Domino

                    Beside the railway tracks a black
frocked priest says Mass, washing the feet of the unabsolved.
On the fronds of coconut trees the spindled light is threshed
into a fire. Moving through space, through time,
the unargued premises of our lives persist. Ascending
carpeted stairs beside alcoves where little mock Roman porcelain
love-gods smile. Breathing the air of the earth. Behind
the high walls of compounds the sonorous voices of children fly,
birds out of foliage. A song returns from the ruined epithalamium
of its past. An aroma of impregnable questions fills our path.
Like a perpetually out of reach pith of sweetness. Over the rails
from the freight-cars comes the smell of condemned flesh.
                                                                Livestock,
hoof deep in piss. Who will stand and say a prayer over them?

Maginhawa Street

The blighted face of a word. Noxious creek.
Dark estuary of lives, washed up. Prostitutes, shoelace
vendors, the occasionally employed. Through
the capital's sempiternal heat they drift, linger, lean against
each other, and then are gone—into another sodden labyrinth
of muddy alleyways, with roofs held on by rocks and
tyres. Here, in this room's cramped shadows, wafts
from under the door an odour of rice-cakes and effluence.
Someone, groaning, stirs at the end of the afternoon
released from a haunting dream of beer or shabu,
and curses. Their ruined discourse drifts by us
on the floor. I feel the warmth of your small waist
in my hands. Emaciated kittens scavenge outside
amid the debris of rotting eggshells and bones.
Old men sleep behind grilles in sari saris their heads abuzz
       with flies:
on shelves behind them the labels on canned fish have curled
and faded in fierce light. Tethered by a length
of string to its leg, a chicken attempts to fly.
Your mouth opens and, in its darkening flesh, glows.
Like stars, your fillings give back the last of the remaining light.

Maginhawa: Tagalog for comfortable

The Stair

You have always been in all of my poems, a secret
odour, an atmosphere, pervading their sound;
of open wounds, of roads going off into sheer light.
In the deepest vicissitudes of their syllables you have promised,
as you pronounced them, pain and joy, trailing behind you,
in room after room, a fragrant pharmacopoeia
of sighs. Dark door of alterity,
the pores of my words open to receive you. You,
who come from far off with the dust of a long journey
on your heels, the expression of indigo skies in your smile.
You watch the wind drive the rain into the eyes
of the sweepstakes ticket buyers on Leon Guinto as if
they are tears, and look at me out
of a lopsided shack of plywood and tin, a dim alleyway
awash with offal and water. Your eyes are alive
with the vocabulary of the living, the dead, and those not yet
born. I carry your dark gaze within me,
an acid eating my flesh, a shard gnawing
my shadow, through streets where poems are written on the façades
of buildings, in brick and dust, and where, in a whitewashed wall,
a thin stone stair climbs perpendicular and,
twisting like a waist near the top, suddenly goes out of view.

The Lovely Cow Dung Flower
(So Nam *1944–94*)

Hurled to the ground,
where you had slipped, or willed
yourself through that open mouth
of appetent air, at, almost
the precise moment of the year's
turning, leaving behind you
son and wife. As I leaf
through your poems now,
our photograph beside
me—a finger from my own
failed marriage tensed
above the shutter—you reinvoke
in the lost fields of Kamtin
your childhood, and you remember
your lost love, your
"life long ambition [so] cruelly
forsaken"—"Suzie, of Morrison
Library at Berkeley, Sun Shine land
Garden of Love." And I wonder
if in this little hill garden
in Yuen Long that you came back
to occupy, you could ever
forget that "radiant Beauty,
unsurpassed Sweetness," slipping
further and further from you.
Love; a continuance,
and an inconvenience, something
to look backward to,
like the lovely cow dung flower
that roots up through
your words, saturated with

the light of those bright fields
of Kamtin, to whose immeasurable
stillness and fullness
you would return, to regain
your lost poise; regained,
and lost a second time! Your unfulfilled
shadow slopes across this page
and I can hear your voice
again in my ear, whispering,
one week out of the asylum, afraid
of your wife. "Please remember
this endearing and enduring
name." Poet to poet,
Tu Fu dreaming of Li Po, I
send these words across that
"overwhelming chasm" to search
for you. "Soul mates for life,"
how could you not hear?

(The quotations are from a translation of Tu Fu's poem 'Dreaming of Li Po' completed by So Nam just before he died, and from the long dedication to Suzie which he appended to it.)

Crepuscular Summer

If you listen hard enough
   you can hear, through the dry
crepuscular sounds of summer, the dead
   butterflies circle in air,
the shadows of a thin
   exhalation. And, under
your hand, rustling the edge
   of sunlight and water,
someone carving your name, on an
   afternoon you cannot quite remember.
Obliterated whole. Letters strung
   together from silence. The broken wall
at the end of a garden,
   the rusting latch of a gate,
the melody half heard
   through an open window;
neither imagined, nor real. Fragments
   you inhale on the desiccated
sward of the years, blown
   back and forwards. A leaking
arcanum. There, amid the smell
   of dead leaves and branches-
the water in a pool
   whose dark skin you break.
It still holds your reflection.

At the 26th University of the Philippines' National Writers' Workshop, Baguio

As if words could recover this light that spills
through the cones of the pine trees.
There is nothing that is so faithful, in the act
of being perceived, that we can record it
with any certainty. Even desire
moves, and fades. And the branches that bend
in the wind make no concession to this
glad virtuosity that threads through everything.
Like anonymous gifts, birds fly in the windows.
The approximate measure of our perceptions falls
before us. A thin light ripples.
                        Our minds are steeped in symbols.

Outside, late afternoon rain beats on concrete
and pine needles. In the wind that blows
through the room, following the birds,
the awkward grammar of a world, its predication,
slowly unfolds on the pages before us.
Texture of tongue, of breath. The unanticipated clause.
Like music, like music, the unrecuperable
sounds of the birds, far off, higher
and higher on the mountain, outrunning the storm.

Uncollected
2000

Between

Plate glass
harbour, reflecting
itself;
meteorological beacon,
observatory.

Contours
vibrate to a sound
of theodolites
incising shape
between windy headlands.

Divisoria drowns
in a fume of gusts,
lacquered grime;
not
in one place
at one time
do we hear ourselves

fully, talking,
thinking, writing
one hand
pressed against
the shadows
of a city, moving

between
sudden alacrity
of grief

and an idea,
through time

dividing
and conjoining. Foliate
desire.
Light filling
the drawing rooms
of the planet,

railway terminuses
with enormous clocks
and, amidst
discord of telephones,
the looks of an abandoned
hope,

waiting. Limpid
conservatories of our childhood
rift beneath us—
upholstered
dreams! The edge
the edge of something

beautiful
we heard,
in a room
or on a beach, its sound
leaving us breathless.

Always at all points
of departure
distance

viaducts, empty fields.
If only,
on the pale parchment
of the hour,
under the streetlight,
we could refract
through pure sounds
the news

of our arrival.
Trembling, with all we know
but cannot name,
indigo ink
of nights drawn down upon us,
looking up

only a tutelage of signs
to ferry us through
the dark matrix
of our selves to what
constructed place,
that could welcome us,
would we come
determinate, and brief
held by
         no other possessions
than these.

from
Belonging
2009

Light Where There Is

A figment
the whole drift
and slew

of air
fricatives colliding
in an empty place

leaves surrender
careless effigies
of who we are

and insistent
light where there is
dark undergrowth

grown daily
more rank
within extremities

of pain   But—
the air unheard
nonchalance pervading

itself and us
caught in the bend
of a wrist

transcribed
topography of sound
giving back what

we never were
can be
The grey face

in a rain of weeks
life dissolving
marls and toxins

And   as if
acacias were bent
shadows from the brim

of some immense
caprice a voice
a silence   It is

more than we deserve
knowing ourselves
so sparely to enun

ciate   So clear
Tides of a factory
scum foul odour

of regret for
things done not
done   Yet

there is
joy simply
in the holding of

words on a page
that do not deliver us
from our selves.

A Habitation

The snowdrops, broken necked on tall stems under the trees have gone. Terracotta sun plaques line the sandstone walls of the courtyard. A curlew falls above a far off meadow. Where do the clouds go, but to the edge of the horizon. We are orphaned almost as soon as we can talk from the wind that leaves no names inside us. The river, a harried sound now over the earth's shoulder, echoes through the panes of the empty summerhouse and beside the drained swimming pool. Each day the sensations of our past come back to haunt us. Broken laughter at the top of steps, a particular look, smell, the angle of light across a face or sward of grass. They hover on the desks at which we sit poring over our dictionaries, catalogues and compendiums, the conduits of a place which we construct. Beyond the sound of all the words is the sound of the air, breathing. An empty road on the brow of a hill defines the limits of our field of vision. Maybe, though, if we were to utter our names again in the wind it would come back without them — having gathered, from these worn out and debilitated siftings, the source of all the names; that deep vacancy and stillness towards which each day the mind, along with the tired echo from the empty summerhouse, bends. And from which the swimming pool drains a slow fosse of light which ripples at the edge, as if it was filling.

The Pear Tree

Irresolute border, the wind shifting in
the hedgerow. Immaculate white lawn of
snow. Pale light moving across the river.

Where a face turned behind a curtain,
refulgent in shadow. Was it the curve of
the mind—the breath's camber—or a real figure.

For daylight's first loss, recorded nothing
but this. Beyond an open window night,
an immeasurable sadness of streets,
filling the intervals of a life.

Glow on buildings, railroads clanking in
the dawn's stillness, the smell of livestock.

And nothing differs, except the difference
of loss and gain. A memory of distinct
horizons and spaces, peopled by a question.

Rockpools. Calendulas in churches.
Tracing a likeness out of despair.

The pear tree filtering—like a great web of
suspended motes—air: looking up into it.

Would solve nothing, landscape, dream
figure that a mind makes, shifting
between itself and that imagined other.

Desire reduced to a brisk metaphor of exchange,
consumed, burned by its own transport.
Damp bodies, gathering sand on the world's littoral.

What we proceed towards
through the night's humidity day's rancour, tinkle
of goat bells across a far river bloom
of white dust upon dead words.

My darkling syllable strung upon a high
cloister, echo I listen for, faded angelus,
fingertap upon my broken window.

Turns, turns the light on in each dark
corner, "In the softly luminous hour tell
me a story, where nothing is more than
itself, an object turning in its own memory."

Is only this: an ember of dusk, caught in
the wind; a shadow that calls to us out
of an aperture in a garden wall, from another country.

Edges

Body that has no country
no map, no horizon to navigate by.
It sets out on,
and is the sole author of,
its own journey.
Unannounced, always
unexpectedly taking off into the blue of elsewhere;
bowsprit, the ideal music
of the purest memories
that have been ground down
into disconsolate atmospheres
in which we are waiting, breathing
the air of some where else.

In the reinstated constituents
of time and space, standing
outside a bookstore, the *Solidaridad*
on Padre Faura, thinking
what is the light doing
looking for a place
in which it could belong, watching
the dust turn ceaselessly
under the acacia trees.

Impermanent blue
shadow,
the treacherous edge
of a 'here'.

The wisp of a wind
would blow it away,
into a sky woven with
promises. It follows us
with the shape of leaking horizons,
the grey impersonations of waves
        that break upon
rooms filled with the saddest
of roses, of old photographs,
a haunting chemistry that blows
from some remote topography:
                          sounds
through an open window
that no one has heard before
or composed.

Place of unconnected moments
of infinite arrivals and farewells,
of a sail on a shore.
Whose is this face that we seem to remember
but can't quite recall:
the discarded fragment of a dream,
perhaps, a melody, intended to lead us
back to where it began.
Half heard conversations.
Unrecuperable names.
They shelve away down
to a broad sunlit avenue,
to trees that ripple
on a white plain
where lightning lacerates a dark sky.

In the stillness of 'not moving'
someone,
suddenly, thinks *home*.
Dark petals
on a sill, a lace
curtain bending in,
corroborate, and mock,
    a sense of being
somewhere else.

Ideal place of memories:
                      glimpsed —
    then gone.

Lisping,
sometimes, in the coordinates
of a lost tongue
it brings back to us
              nothing
but the kapoc tree at night in bloom
and the shadow of the one
who passed under it,
at noon, muttering
who am I, carving
his signature out of the wind.

A Boyhood

Not a sound
through the dark
air only
a dog barking
click of a dynamo
on spokes, before sleeping

house fronts.
Cold latches.
Environs, barred
to him. Days
held in the element
of despair, floated

up a hill
past the wooded
moat of sky. To
where, and who,
beyond himself,
was watching, if at all

the land forming
round a question,
river moving
through its treacherous sediments,
Shoreditch, Purfleet, Gravesend,
while the marsh burned

white flesh from stalks
and the church threw
its pointed shadow across the vigour of
a dead pastoral. Ominous
succession of signs; words

to denigrate
the shape of the tongue, stuttering
father's employment, school.
Supineness before authority.
'The best infantry in the world.'
He heard

the afternoon sigh
on the ragged verges
of council estates,
where the shop fronts creaked out of their
broken names and hoardings

'Alston, Edwards, Nunn,'
generations that stayed,
and the light, pouring
through orchards and graveyards,
and birdsong. Journeys, beginning

and ending,
a twilight
of narratives. Where
the river moved
amid the summer spores,
nettles and dockleaves

through small creeks,
trickled, he wrote
his name
upon the softened stump
of a rotting aspen
branch, and launched it.

Belonging

    To no where
to no thing
to the shortest abridgement
of air   of word
to   the cruel insignia
          of our acquisitions.

Lost
under damp swamp of cloud
      muddy field
           the moon
's light
      very first embrace.
Still missing.

The scent of what lies
  at the end of the road;
    a copse
of guava trees, perhaps,
      or tamarind:
  suffused in the wind,
gathering   and dispersing.

Flame
      in windless rain
that keeps   burning

                    hand
of the one who doubts.
                            The sound
of a pure line of thought   running
      carrying over
                     into the present.
Beside the table   a blue chair
         with all the confidence of
               a disclosure
leaning into space
         and silence.

To no particular
   time   or place
         then.
Under the shadow   of the rain trees
      I saw her hurrying
towards what
                    was only
a distant speckle of light
   upon a   possible event.

               Heard
     in the rustle of
that air,   as it was
                    departing,
another moment   arising.
         A history
of burned pages.

  Cannot come back
    cannot, ever,
       return to
   where it was,
       crushed between
  those pale linens
       a sprig
  of purple sweetening
    the tongue.

    Was
  the width of a breath
  between us, crossing
   the hot courtyard,
      unable to compose
  ourselves through all those
    annihilations
  we had not spoken of
   over which we
  had no control.

  The dark saxifrages,
   in a crevice
  on a slope, bending
   in the breeze
  of a bright morning
      having,

             unlike ourselves,
                          no need
     to locate
just where they are.

Move
       across
    this sandstone wall
         this acropolis of air
your voice
             so that the emptiness may spall
                        and stain
          into it.

     For
what we are
             excluded from,
         the roots' white
                  intricate knot,
                  air
through the thin shadows of our bodies
              refutes,
         grinding the rocks
under our feet   dissolving
the black ashes of words
     in our throats.

Signifies only
    what it does not
        possess
but will go on   looking
    for
among all the vagaries and evaporites
    that attend it
        leaving
in this trackless dust
    a footprint,
    the pale ghost
of a voice
        crossing a road.

Archipelago Nights

Bone white sheen,
and she has slipped
quietly away
from you in sleep,
the phosphorescence
of a shallow lingers
wide, enveloping
arm, leg

                      antiphon
of doomed corals,
a submerged republic
that rides up onto
the waters of the night,
bring back voices
over the surf, into
this quiet

                      who
shuffling back, late
from that shore
of lost spirits,
wasted no time
in enfolding, street
by street, an entire
imago, the chaos
of your life, in her mind

                      a skull
of forsaken memories,
emporia of dreams, where

remains of the displaced
and the exploited grip
the eyes' ebb, flight
towards another coast
that's unenveigled, transparent

                             gauging
the precise angle
of the head and feet, the
body's disposition, waits
among the abaca and
the looms of shipwrecked
hands, and dances,
though the signs
are not propitious

                             speaks
out of the dried up
reservoirs, the slums
of bought-off voters, declining
to name the price
of silence, her hands
arranging the wreathes
of victims, spread
and undressed

                         binds,
with a calla lily,
the broken waist
of the water,

a bracelet of tiny scars
round her wrist,
the blood of indentured labourers
on haciendas
darkening her streams

                          drawn
into each small
hollow, cove, breathing
an exile's prayer,
the filth of clogged esteros
filling the streets,
you wait,
uneasily, on the night's
escarpment of bone

                 where
flotsam, gulls,
and driftwood meet
the horizon, level
with the edge
of some glittering repose,
the heart pounds
solitary, moving
between itself and others,

                        clear
light of moon
to navigate you through
reefs, drawing

around you a fleet of ghosts,
words —*land reform*,
abolition of oligarchy—
tilling air
to see
what will grow
on shifting current.

                              Thin
like a wafer,
they dissolve
upon the tongue …
indigent's breath,
crepuscular
flower of the retreating
jungle, invoking them
you invoke yourself,
again

amidst a catafalque
of blooms, of horns.
In desolate barrios, bound for foreign
aquariums, the doomed
corals of the republic
raise, like bleached bone,
their branches up
into an air in which
they drown.

Uncollected
2001

from The Fragrant Emporia

Because of the hurried and unending train of his discourse I was not able to reliably identify the names of the places in which he had stayed. Discomposed by the intensity of his gaze I looked at his shadow, suffused with the odour of Gitanes, and listened. "Time never stops. From within time how do we know anything, except what is provisional. Each letter longing to unite with a word, each word with a sentence, and that sentence—a miracle!—to stand, finally, on its own."

...   ...

Lost in the backward pull of what we have left; memories, possessions—death's shadow over us. They are siren voices. The black swell under the bright froth of the wave that sucks us down into an antechamber of stale echoes in which we will search for something that is not there. On the flight back a Lebanese merchant, a textile manufacturer from Beirut, who had studied in his country, looked into his eyes and said: "I don't think that after having lived in this continent for so many years you will be able ever to live again in your own country."

...   ...

In the silence of hotel lobbies you can still hear them, he remarked sadly, travelling through time, their unobliterated footsteps on marble laid down millions of years ago, their travelling bags heavy with samples and orders, their deodorized shadows caught in the glass walls of atriums like fleeting forms trapped in amber. Tedious merchants of conversations, carrying, somewhere deep within themselves, the chemistry of ancient atmospheres, of uninscribed horizons, their pink chins dappled with light refracted through thousands of identical rooms.

.

The inebriated instruments of the indigenous musicians at a pension of lice and shadows. Dung in the alleyways. A subservient populace. Escape into sound! He inhaled the asbestos of burned down factories. Sirens of police raiding down side streets, looking, in a ruined economy, to supplement their official pittances. All night a litany of drinks filled his glass. In the mornings they sought him out with a pornography of tears and he dozed, sometimes, unknown to them, in the dark while the projector flared. In the evening the toil of fragrant arms. By a harbour of stinking refuse the light burned to a deep pulsating blue. Avenues of sauntering bodies under the sagging power lines. The dust of white, mahogany shaded, village roads at dusk. And, somewhere, that elusive, and slightly shy, crepuscular smile of a youth. A wild mouth cupped in the dark, full of the sweetness of an uncorrupted source.

……

There was only sadness left in the arcades of desire. The statues' taut pressure lines of skin over muscle and bone were elaborated in the smile, or gravitas, of the statuary of the living. One night as he came back across the river, counting the bridges all the way down the dark, weed choked, estuary, he thought that the tide had left without him. Swarms of white ants, in the humid tropical night, flocked against the windscreen shedding their wings, and wriggling away. As the car stopped and he opened the door, he realised that it was a dream, and that no ship was waiting for him … They do not constitute us, the objects of our waking and unwaking, he thought.

You can go only so far, and then you can go no further. Wielding titles and diplomas in empty places. Scanning the horizon for another area to annex, or explore. The seas come up to you and wet the sky blue of your garment. What else is there to do, but disappear. Folded in the purest air of the invariant, the intervals of grasses and of books. The noise of wars. The sounds of amorous advances. In the half light he read the score of a child's music that was fading in and out of each refuge where he had sought some solace from a life of failure. Among the spines of gilded libraries. Among all conceptualizations. And, in his mouth he ran his tongue around, instead of words, the perfect and bitter roundness, the oblation, of silence.

www.ingramcontent.com/pod-product-compliance
Lightning Source LLC
Chambersburg PA
CBHW031149160426
43193CB00008B/307